NEWS F
THE BRIGHT(

Also by Nicki Jackowska

Poetry
The House that Manda Built
(The Menard Press 1981)
Earthwalks
(Ceolfrith Press 1982)
Letters to Superman
(Rivelin Grapheme 1984)
Gates to the City
(Taxus Press 1985)

Fiction
Doctor Marbles and Marianne – A Romance
(Harvester 1982)
The Road to Orc
(Bran's Head Books 1985)
The Islanders
(Harvester 1987)

NEWS FROM THE BRIGHTON FRONT

Nicki Jackowska

SINCLAIR-STEVENSON

First published in Great Britain by
Sinclair-Stevenson Limited
7/8 Kendrick Mews
London SW7 3HG, England

Copyright © 1993 by Nicki Jackowska

All rights reserved.
Without limiting the rights under copyright reserved,
no part of this publication may be reproduced,
stored in or introduced into a retrieval system or transmitted,
in any form or by any means (electronic, mechanical,
photocopying, recording or otherwise), without the prior
written permission of both the copyright owner
and the above publisher of this book.

The right of Nicki Jackowska to be identified as author
of this work has been asserted by her in
accordance with the Copyright, Designs and Patents Act 1988.

British Library Cataloguing in Publication Data
A CIP catalogue record for this book is available from the British Library.
ISBN 1 85619 306 3

Typeset by Rowland Phototypesetting Limited
Bury St Edmunds, Suffolk
Printed and bound in Great Britain
by Clays Limited, St Ives plc

For Laura

ACKNOWLEDGEMENTS

Some of the poems have appeared previously in the following magazines: *Ambit, Aquarius, Foolscap, Giant Steps, London Magazine, The North, Outposts, Phoenix Review* (Australia), *Poetry Durham, Poetry Review, The Rialto, Stand, Women's Review, Words International* and *Writing Women.*

Some of the poems have appeared previously in the following anthologies: *Angels of Fire* (Chatto & Windus), *Dancing the Tightrope* (The Women's Press), *Home and Away* (Southern Arts, ed. Carol Ann Duffy), *P.E.N. Anthology II* and *Purple and Green* (Rivelin Grapheme).

'She Tries' and 'August Thief' appeared in Nicki Jackowska's first collection, *The House That Manda Built* (The Menard Press, 1981), and 'Un-Fairytale' and 'Ship Out of Water' appeared in her third collection, *Letters to Superman* (Rivelin Grapheme, 1984).

'News from the Brighton Front' was read by Nicki Jackowska on TVS' *Artbeat* in 1989. 'Farewell to Brighton' was read by her on *Time for Verse* and also as part of her appearance on the *South Bank Show* production, *The Literary Island*, transmitted by Channel Four, July 1991.

Contents

I: UNMINDFUL

Unmindful	3

II: AVOCADO

Getting There	7
Cutting	9
A Question of Resistance	11
Catch	12
Romany	13
Avocado	14

III: DON'T LOOK NOW

Don't Look Now	17
This Noon	19
A Narrow-Gauge Railway	20
Scratch of a Rusty Nail	21
Gorple	22
Moonshot	23
House of Usher	24
Simone's Cat	25
Old Gold in Colne	26

IV: AFRICAS

Tiger	31
Africas	33
Don't Speak the Language	34
Opening the River	35

V: NEWS FROM THE BRIGHTON FRONT

News from the Brighton Front	39
Matanzas in the Bath Arms	44
Empty in the Sleazy City	46
Reducing the Dose	47
Farewell to Brighton	48

VI: FEVERS

Un-Fairytale	51
She Tries	52
August Thief	53
Cut-Glass Punchbowl	54
Fevers	56
Zodiac	58
Making a Season	59

VII: CONCERNING THE ALLOTMENT

Concerning the Allotment	63
Fault	64
Crossings	65
The Company She Keeps	66
Breaking Waves	67
Out of the City	68
Simone Dances	69

VIII: LETTERS WITHOUT PAPER

Letter from the Terrace	73
Vendetta	75
Music on Victoria Station	76
Power Houses of Lumb Bank	77
Ship out of Water	78
The Fiction-Maker	79
Figure-Flasher, You Been Here Before	80
Letters without Paper	81

IX: A PROUD SHORE FOR LEGENDS

A Proud Shore for Legends	85

I: UNMINDFUL

Unmindful

At six o'clock I turned on the television
to watch the six o'clock news
and to my surprise there appeared in full colour
a picture of Mount Olympus, and the gods
arrayed in all their splendour one above the other.
Then I saw that Zeus was looking a little peculiar.
He'd obviously had a sex-change or liked
dressing up as a woman. His wreath of golden laurel
looked curiously like a dried and frizzy wig
and why was he dressed in a blue suit and a false bosom
waddling across a bleak street and not
enshrined on his mountain. And why did he stand
in the posture of a warrior, but the words coming out
fell like chips of wood and clattered on the steps
of Downing Street. I did not understand.
Zeus seemed somehow to have slipped out of his clothes
and gone walk-about. You can see warts
on his chin and his Olympian team
look all the same. Their spears must be hidden
in those oblong black slabs they carry in their hands
and the sky wears a flat white veil like a shroud.
So I decide to write a letter to the gods
and send it care of the British Broadcasting Corporation
in case the camera had a warp in the lens
or perhaps my set wants tuning, or I've put
my contact lenses into the wrong eyes
and the world's turned upside-down. Perhaps that
hole in the road is Olympus in reverse
and Zeus is lying at the bottom of a well
his voice a long way off, so all you hear
is the faintest echo of what a man or woman
(who can tell which is which) might once have been.

II: AVOCADO

Getting There

I couldn't remember the name of the band
or the pub, or the man I am supposed to love,
stepping out on Saturday against the black wall
of the London road at night, only a slight
tug at the umbilical when we passed the pet-shop
where we'd found baskets, flaps and collars –
clever confinements for our regressive cat.
And I remembered my husband's lean hand
calming the fur, as I lay all riddled,
shrunken after a journey; and how the house
settled like a cloak on me and had me back –
masked it's true, but then our skin defies
disguises and small indulgencies poke through.

Passing the darkened pet-shop and the laundry
memory didn't know its place, pierced pin-holes
in the bland sheet-lighting of the London road
as though someone shoved a hot thin needle
in my breast and pulled it out again, so fast
the quick sting had no time for recognition.
We leaned against the wind and found the venue
beyond the Co-op, undertakers and the Oxfam shop.
A man with a squeeze-box and an eager beard
whisked the air a little with his songs
that didn't stretch into our fidgety laps
but fell like tired birds wounded in the nest.
Then the band came on, swept up the dead
and turned our sleeping genius inside out.
I always wanted skinny arms, a body hanging
lank and white inside a bleached vest, as though
all colour leapt to her head; the fiddler worked
her bow, as I do late at night when the moon teases
you to death, your linen shining like the ice-cap,
a great white eye that's almost fit to blind you.
Sylvia is here, and Laura glowing in her self-embrace
arms hooked on each other for neither love nor money,

caging a fancy shirt that beams its pattern out
to keep her heart from too close dance, too early.

A hand-rolled cigarette gleams on the wood
next to my glass; Sylvia's wearing Jasper Conran,
a mine of silver at the neck, falling like ransom.
And yet her bush of hair curls like tobacco.
I hold this thin cigarette as a rare purchase,
light it up, knowing the rasp and kick of where
we came from and where we might be going.
Smoke across the fiddler's bones, her arching throat.

Cutting

*for Jurek and Isa, lace-workers
of Nottingham*

Nottingham

From his terrace he hears
mountain's bell-sound carving the rockface
wide span measuring his thumb's hook.
He cradles scissors close
as once her breast spilled there.

Now white, his flesh is lace
this fist of wedding-trim
erupting from the chair's lap.

Like sheep he sheds his
spilled heart's colour, drains
his miniature in one draught

all the wide air syphoned
down the street, blowing lace
roses like a puffball

all in his name's wake.

Leschaux

Master of none, he pads his hotel
terrace; does not lace the mountain
in his day's net, lets it ring.

Above him in the worn hill's
cleft, lodges a hero's monument
men felled above the treeline.

Threads on his window-ledge
stems of the pass; when you
cut lace the two streams part
in scalloped bridal-skirts, regular
white rhythms of the circular.

Cutting for marriage; then the
fall of trimmings, spare cloth
on the mountain close to fleece.

When you cut, the path does not
return; we came down from the peak
unstitching shells and roses.

Foxglove on the grave sparking
their withered stalks;
so does the blade resist.

A Question of Resistance

I remember
the house I first quickened
its night-pace, its stars
the fold of dawn across unblemished
sheets, the leniency.

I remember
walking the bare hill
with a hard bald heart
and heels ready
for this winter tenancy.

And how you slipped inside
between one story
and its issue, how you
did not mistake the turning

slid hawk-eyed to my side
and lodged against the hill
to see you through.

It's been a tough season
one might almost say
unnatural, except that I

confess to truancy, absent
without leave a full year
before your books and brains
and your sly raw hands

took flight; light your own
fire, you said, the child put out.
Whose, I don't know; it came quick
and dark between us like a blade.

Catch

I woke up in the middle of the night
on Wednesday the eleventh of October
in the small hours, when blackness sinks
low in the belly and your ears are like
bright steel rods that wave in the room for clues.
And I heard this sound between my legs
in the wild land there, that was never husbanded,
land left to graze and scattered with small scrub bushes.
As I listened, it seemed that many tiny fists
were beating on my inner walls
hammering with their soft knuckles on the slithery
passages I've learned to blaze and also
to be wary of; so hearing that gathering population
thunder in there, as though storm brooded
way off over the Beacon, where night is a little
madder than I am, a little redder at the rim,
I know that my children call to me from their cells
fisting for life, angry and dumb with their fish-mouths
not to be carved by the good air, into human.
My children call, all the red patches in the room
seem lit, as though a lamp switched on
which shows only red – the poppy stitched
on a tapestry cushion, the scarlet wax run loose,
my shoe, my shoe tilted heavenwards,
all glowing in the night's burn-out, completed.
My eyes are fearful of these finished things
clamouring their craft. I say to all my lost ones,
love, hard to believe, and harder still to catch
allowed you out – too soon, too soon upon the
world's clasp, you had no tools to swim with.
I say to them, I love you still, my fish, my
                                        unborn warriors.

Romany

Through the rooks, through the stalks of trees
a gold and silver horseshoe piercing my doorstep
like a nail. Her voice is hammered through
in winter and luck comes sneaking in between
the door-frame and confusion, where daffodils
are out and dead before they know it.

She says the things I want to hear and yet
it's taking several minutes to create her all
of a piece, as she mouths the fragments
of a life that could be mine, scatters
my heart from its mould like lucky heather.

She had a fiver out of me testing the need.
Having no property she teases out the corner
of my eye a landless carelessness,
plucks the fiver from a palm which
promises long life. New out of marriage
I come running, to wonder if the ring
I never wore winks like a bitten horseshoe
in the light; I pass her visit off as
superstition, but desire is merciless.
A small limb aches like a phantom finger,
                              never clothed.

Avocado

He left an avocado in the fridge
I took it out and held it, felt it plump and soft
carried the coffin out of last night's dream
and ate the pear he left behind; then roamed the bleak
   forest
like a randy goat, there where our winter ghosts are out.

I ate the avocado my husband left me
and took to the loose woods with a perfect vagabond
hugged in my last year's scarf, biting the wind's ice
out in the new-made raw, half-in half-out of dream
the day that never quite launched itself into the light.

We kept our fists hard-balled in worthy jackets
and I am used to fencing with the dark so snipe and
circle through the bare trunks skinned of last year.
The sky presses down, and so we tramp. I have you
in my eye's pocket where the flotsam gathers
deep in the seam. I have you where you tell me
that your house bears old lace, cinnamon, the wide-eyed
island where you grew; and I could marry you
were it not for all that dead wood.

As for me I believe I lodge in the crevice of your root
between my clever angles, where the woods slide
out of sight, eased like that coffin in my dream
last night, we carried back, back to the old worn room
we fell from. There, we said to the assorted family
there is the glowing box its coals alight; see how we
carry it this far and merrily, see how our hands clasp
over the split fruit, green and ripe.

III: DON'T LOOK NOW

Don't Look Now

Don't look now
the door is opening on a tête-à-tête
fine wire between the parties
her foot one step upon his flight
he leaning like an angel in a bright shirt
tugging at their cord.

Don't look now
as though to say come on (he says)
playing with light
(and don't attend the company)
time splintering at his neck
her hands there ache.

Don't look, don't look
the crack between the door's extension
and its close, is large enough.
She's caught there on the phone
watching the slit
and don't, the world parts so
its yawn erupting from the mouth
and billowing gaunt and toothless
down the line to take her daughter
(what, what is it, do speak soon)
and then the wild world's lap.

Soon and still soon his flesh, the
valley and the meal are hurly-burlied
round the walls cutting their proofs.
The house flies apart, don't look.
National Geographics fly from the attic
the pavement's spattered with aduki beans
and they lie in each sparse bed jammed
in the door's foot, wondering how
a casual visitor could reap such harvest.

All fall down the nursery says
the child wills it, the pincer-grip
of pain; the need to have the
whole lot out and grinning.

Don't look now
blood and red wine, the spilled country
mock-cavity walls, light splicing through
the lie of what is seen freeze-frame
and out of joint; her hero mangled
in the twinkling of an eye.

This Noon

Leaving the greyhaired man, beloved urchin
still in his night-cast face
she, the poet, didn't come so far this time
and didn't make a virtue out of it.

Leaving him standing blue and burnt
in the door's shaft, her house shifted
north north-west and grew a tongue
that is forever sounding for his name.

A Narrow-Gauge Railway

A gloved hand in my lap
and metal sparks among the ice
splintering its glaze.
In the carriage a chorus of breaths
steaming up the glass, spinning
a veil across white mountain's crest.

A child crooks her finger to
the window, carves a bold heart.

Slowly our train inches along the ridge
tilted to sky; we dare not look.
Land plunges from these thin rails
like a suicide.

Too hard you tell me, (without a word)
your voice a needle's eye I can't squeeze through,
can't ride the ridge you sketch each night,
arrow-track channelled between your legs.
I sprawl (you say) across a fitful range
leaping the peaks, pumping my beer
and smoke, freezing my brain with
endless intermission.

Too vast I say (without a word)
I'm holding tight-arsed in my carriage
daring the narrow gauge; if I pull
the fingers of the glove, expose a hand
within that compass, I'll bite enough.

His face spreads wide across the same
horizon as the mask splits; notch in
the track's rise, meeting a perfect stranger
between one peak and another.

Scratch of a Rusty Nail

Face carved sharp as a mollusc
somewhere to climb, turn, re-align
(like a bay window speaking of sideways).

The car drives sheep before it, country lane
windowless; you let down your rage like hair
somewhere to burst through, cutting corners.

The Cornish hedgerow bears a scar
like the track of a rusty nail; we sit
forever in the trough between two pens.

Across the lane, eggshells and plasm
sticking my hair together as though, beneath,
the brain would spill rotten like old fish.

I write it, your race across me rusty
a blue car still intact but sideways-on
(not like the window), a road closed.

Gorple

And we returned to the foursquare page
again, again where the journey is begotten.
I am not well-armed having cut spinach
last week and picked these few chicken-bones.
But you, ambitious, want the whole
Titanic up and all its populations.
Yet I am told by years and expeditions
it is not wisdom to restore the wreck.

And we fall back into the foursquare bed
and close ranks; and I must visit, touch
the bald rock's slant, feel where its tilt
might tumble me, hear the wind beyond you
and each love's impudence; yet it is not
so, it was not like that. We did not speak
of this, only set it loose among our flesh
and grasses, leaning easy at the gaunt rock's grip.

Moonshot

Reaching out to trespass on that ice-sheet
where you are not; only the moonlight
spreading fins across me, and where
should looking end if I go out
and tramp the lawn's mud down
at night, when you have peeled away
your selves and curled alone upstairs
or in the hollow of a northern hill.

What then I sing alone will call
the moonlight in and rocking over all
the bed, heat it where you are not
and dance alone for all the world's light.
Bare feet on an untreated lawn, seeding
it late, the grass unruly, tufted.
I crouch and moan under these dead trees
and hope for lightning, roar from the sky.

This morning's catalogue inches its nifty
t-shirts round my skin, a subtle moon-shade
in the knit; going out was just to
catch the edge of where I am not.
Now the silk flood of a clever shirt
pulls down torrents, she clutches at his
saxophone wearing white spots; my fingers
ply the page, try last night on for size.

House of Usher

You write of eggshells.
Once this man, his face riddled with
archipelagos, cracked like fine bone
as though he wore
the opposite of armour-plate
beneath his leather.

I am tethered in this house
and wait for bells; these letters ring
their spaces into a tight-balled eye
hunting the ghost of Christmas past
and the house shifts.

What slithers through is not what I
had learned; the rucksack canvas groans.
Let me tell you (who I have not met)
that my old lizard slips his tongue
along a fine hairline, and he will do.

My house is falling and we scratch
the rock for new intentions.

I write to you (with no cartography)
about a man I met whose hide is
slipper-thin, who meets the world's emporium
unforsworn, his letters granular
his lizard-eye tuned bright.

This year I learn foundations,
remember the story. Not quite
gothic my house but trying its small
dramatic monologue, falling and
falling with less than gothic splendour
split like a speckled egg.

I turn it upside-down, pretending
knowing full well there is no patchwork
for the chicken, or for us.

Simone's Cat

At midnight he telephones
rips the line with a kiss.
Sneaks in her hinterland where
father lurks, the year's wedge
lodging in her throat.

So you see she can't sing
all the while he's fish, flipping
a tail in her face, or wolf
in the full moon pretending to
gobble her, forgetting grace.

Hear how she howls at midnight
the largest of cats; a scratch
on the moon's face, a rift
the load of Pendle Hill weighting
her down for the song's catch.

At midnight he telephones.
She curls in her chair like
cellophane, imagines her claw's
claim on Pendle; the rabble
dance him crazy in her mind's
                        immortal eye.

Old Gold in Colne

When he picked me up at the station
his lips brushed mine as though
he were passing on,
as though he were already going
somewhere else. And my lips in turn
what could they do but wriggle like party-fish
sadly in the cold air left behind
in the cold northern air of his passing.

It wasn't always like this.
Once my arrival at the station
in the northern town (sometimes snow on my coat)
was like standing on the most solid stone
I have ever landed on, so deep
it supported me all the way down
from Australia, where father is.
And I know that I must say goodbye
to daddy, there where the skins
part company even in their join.

The cold wind of Christmas whittles in
between the skin father once wore for me
when mine got burned and raw from the bones
crying, and the skin of the man I have
attended these four years and more
battling his peace and his warrior in a round
dance here in the north close to Pendle.

He's clawed the woman who lives up the lane
once too often, one too many knots
like a boy-scout eager to please
in her plush and peach graveyard
her nest of singing snakes near Pendle.
I stuck pins in but it did no good
and now I'm cold of care
with the tracks' rattle and splendour
gone down at sunset to old gold.

And I think of someone I saw last week
reading poems in a peacock shirt,
new blaze of hope out of London's slag-grey.
I think of a man I saw last week
whose hook dangled and snagged in my
new silk stockings (peeled on for winter)
in case that fisherman on the bare bank
should stretch an arm across the picnic-cloth
of forty years, and stroke just so the inner thigh
and so would steal my skin and wear it for me
once again, as my lips brush past this cheek
and open their hearts to the raw westerly, coming
                              up fresh.

IV: AFRICAS

Tiger

In the corner an old sailor is dreaming of tigers
in red weather. She would like to open his face
and let them out. She knew once what it meant to
be tiger, how you could crouch low on the ground,
fierce and ready.

It was a long time ago.

In the corner an old sailor is dreaming of the heart
of darkness, is dreaming of where the path mates with
jungle, is dreaming of land pitched against him, and
how the sky was bloody with torn hide.

His eyes fold back.

She watches the sailor dreaming in the corner in
red weather, flare of a flower-head out of the green
thick as lava.

The jungle boils.

She has never been to the jungle. She would not
survive there. Her feet are not hard for tracking.
She'd sniff her own death too near, always
approaching.

What does it mean to be like him, an old sailor
dreaming of tigers. You watch and remember the
animals under the stair. The lair of dream, the
way something catches you out ready to pounce even
now. Is it called tiger? Does it belong to
sailors?

In the corner an old man meeting his beasts. Perhaps
his hand clenches now sniffing the darkness, feeling
the animal near. Perhaps he is conjuring all the
crouching jungle in his pale eye.

In the corner she writes of an old man. Her coat is red. Tiger is dream, is a word in her book. He crouches ready to meet whoever will conjure him.

Africas

This doll beats his drum.
If this doll came of grass he would
tramp the field down.
But he is root-crop, blade-hidden.

If this doll asks, how shall I answer?
He makes time curl out of his belly
like a dark snake.

If I ask this doll, how is his tongue made
will it have time to spell the hours
of his dancing, before the scythe dips?
Which time will he choose for his saying?

This doll beats her drum.
The sound is locked in.
Shall I ask of her land a different
colour, a basin of dreams.

She thrusts out her breasts and speaks.
How are they carved, parted across
the table, how are they twin.

Don't Speak the Language

The world shrinks to a truck.
On a dusty Lagos road
he spatters his seed among the women
and takes a carved souvenir
an ebony woman-head
home to his wife

and a snakeskin bag
skinning the forest

and a thick silver snake-ring
through which the land slips easy.

Living with contradiction, he says
the women need the dollars.

Look at the sullen bitch.

She's dumb mahogany on his mantelpiece
lopped limb of wood, she's quite translated.

Opening the River

Today I am woman coming to the edge of water
to wash linen caked with dust. How the air resists
my thighs, pushing through. How water clasps me
blue at the foot, white froth on my raking hand.

I haven't been here before, this bowl of water.
The trees are talking thin today. I don't know
how the rinsing water is dissolving threads,
my legs are water-quiet, pitched against flood.

Lifting like sacrifice, the basket creaks wide with sun
its clothes stiffened with earth, their spines crack.
Water sparking out of clay, my shoulder is a bending
hollow; when I enter, river holds there smiling.

V: NEWS FROM THE BRIGHTON FRONT

News from the Brighton Front

The man takes a stone.
He grunts. A chip flies from its flank.
He mixes metaphors.
It winks blue and purple under the crazy pier.

The woman takes a stone.
Its blue skin is startled by her scarlet nail.
She traces a name in its cool fist.
The letter grumbles on her bag's seabed.

Between her feet, sea gnashes, her silver heel
knocks on wood. Waterskin catches her face,
throws it back. Only fish have tunnel vision.
She strolls the pier tossing her hooks overboard.

Honeyman eating candyfloss in a blue striped
blazer. Honeyman in a check suit that yells
summer. Honeyman with nothing in his pockets,
tilted like a liner, waving to the fat thighs
with a pale unburned hand.

You are all used up, she tells the fruit-machine.
Orange peel shredded from the sun's fracture.
Man under the pier tied up with string. Sun
sticking his limbs together. Soon his face will
shine out of its bag, thirsty for fruit.

The woman sees that he is thirsty.
She asks him the time. A watchface spins
in his eye's cyclone. I never stay long
enough, he says.
An hour crawls between her legs. She leaves
him straddled on the weedy groyne.

Going hunting. The crazy pierstakes.
Hunting a crack in the day. Through which
he may pour fish-oil and sweat and the voice
of a romping sea.
Going hunting. Trying to escape from his
string vest. Looking for tunnels into the
light. Her skirts up round the motorway.
It winks blue as a stone.

The man is selling monkeys. Their felt jackets
shout at the strollers like parakeets. Pavements
hot as a jungle. The monkeys chatter, wondering
at the origin of species. Ice-cream runs from
their mouths like the tongues of lilies.
Summer spilling.

The sea wakes first, a thin silver needle.
Then the man breathes earth in through paper
shoes. On the promenade, in the white hotel,
she wakes next in her ruffled bed.
Her sheets itch.

At coffee time she sits in her deckchair
reading the penguin book of contemporary
beetroot recipes.

I've reached rock-bottom she tells her friend,
he's gone back to his wife. The gull flies
too high screaming in ecstasy. He has the
wings for it.

Another fish says her friend, another
pale face coming up out of the tank.
What kind do you want in this aquarium,
dogfish or razoreel. They swim the
promenade, noses against glass.

Who needs a Martian eye. Or uncut videos.
Behind the roasting knuckle, each sunbather
preserves an inwardness of palm. Where the
world tickles in.

The Grand Hotel is missing a couple of floors,
a gash in its proud flank.
Sightseers along the promenade, missing a
couple of floors.
Between the death and the death, a lift-shaft
of silence.
Nostalgic rubble hastily shuffles into
the gap.

Boadicea rides again. Roll up!
Her warship cleaves the tired seafront air. The
papers drum up an audience, slot another cylinder
into the penny machine. Cheap at the price.
And the land has a hole in its flank and water
in her leaky shoes.

Marks and Spencers rise to the occasion. Fly a
drip-dry flag. At seven am he pats the pocket
of his silk pyjamas. No credit card. Still the
shirts fly from cellophane to comfort him and
blouses drift across well-heeled breasts to
comfort him.
We do not hesitate to clothe our leaders, says
the manager, unlocking his plate-glass doors
two hours early.

Money down the drain, down the penny-machine,
pouring from the till.
Someone reverses the video and Marks and Spencers
clothes the cabinet. Consolation for a hole in
the side.
We are glad the emperor has a new suit of clothes
says the manager, stroking his assets and his
salesgirl with a shot-silk paw.

She has a hole in her bag where the letter falls
through and her boss pays for the orchestra to play
her evening wide, and the hole in the white hotel
says the critic is where the sightseers crowd on in,
too many of them, the ship splits a seam and begins
its slow march to the sea-bed.

Do not go naked into the conference chamber,
clothe the cabinet of curiosities, speciality
of Brighton, the museum preserves a discrete
shade.

Moving towards winter. Beginning to gather, tanks
on the pierhead in spite of clement weather.
Woman in indian summer deckchair reading of penguins.
Behind her the Grand Hotel with a hole in its face.
Behind her Boadicea with a hole in her heart. Behind
her the president, a hole in his celluloid.

I don't like this movie, he says, there's a frame
missing where the people ought to be.
Someone left the Indians on the cutting-room
floor.

Behind her the Grand Hotel where leaders danced
waving their gilt-edged securities. Someone said
they're the guardians of the British way of life.
Which is also to say brutal wish to lacerate, or
bomb with love, or even best writers of lies.
She prefers boastful witnesses of limpets, having
one stuck to her shoe. And writes it.

Graffiti under the pier. They're surprised when
the shadows speak, these leaders, it interrupts
the pantomime. Thought Indians were extinct, won't
they ever learn, we're in charge of the cutting-room
floor.

Stone-scratchers that rise up against the town's
cataract and cut its blind face.
It takes an operation to remove a root.

In charge of summer, winter, and in charge of
words for it. The postcard flies in the teeth
of the ice-cap on the other side.
Though her skin's still seasonal.
It hits the president on the chin. He swats
a fly.

In Gatsby-under-Wold he leans to adjust the silver
nipple of his radio set. In Brighton she stretches
to turn down the volume of fish-sound that keeps
escaping from aquariums.
Between them, a continent rises. They give each
other credit for not creating it.
Decide not to consult over the means of exploration.

In the early hours of friday october twelve nineteen
eighty-four, gulls scatter. She wakes in her bed
at two forty-five and asks him if he's locked the
car. The timer creeps to zero, the end of dialogue.
The prime minister leaves the bathroom and launders
her speech. You can smell salt in the backstreets.
He and she fuck across the distances.
They say the fuse was set a century ago.

Matanzas in the Bath Arms

I'm sitting in the amber shadows of the Bath Arms
the window behind me yellow, wrinkled like ancient skin
and my beer sparking the sun's light deep in its vat.
During that lunchtime stroll to the bar and back
I've tipped over the edge of today's fortress,
swung on my own rope across the moat and landed
in front of him, my hand held out for blessing.
It didn't take long for conversation to prickle
into life; the barman clears my ashtray every time
I twist an empty crisp-packet into a pig's tail
catching the slow whirl of alcohol across the brain
from one ear to another; then the pub's pantomime,
how they drift and posture, how the mid-day punters
sink a pint. Collars shift uneasy on their necks
among the niggle and spite of this one hour's grace.
And the girls together lean on each other's eyes
for confirmation. The barman hovers, executes careful
ballets according to my progress down the glass.
And on the third day he arabesques across my tracks
bloodless spectacles slipping a touch on the bridge
and tells me of Majorca, the flat he owns there
close to the shore, and the high citadel where Chopin
lingered on the terrace, spilled his exquisite notes
to catch the moment's ache between one deepening
indigo and another; I tell him I was there once
on that same hiatus, trying to forge a sensibility
outside my father's frame. He talks of ritual,
the pig they slaughter, slitting the throat
the hulk up-ended to drip his passion out.
And into the Bath Arms steals another music
of the dying beast, his frantic eye, blood pouring
scarlet seams across the carpet and its unlit faces.
The barman turns to sepia, mouthing his tale.
They call it *matanzas*, he says, *matanzas* when he dies.
I hear scorched earth hissing beneath the pig,
shriek of a vessel loosing its life too fast.

Matanzas, he says, pulling the pump, a golden liquid spouting merrily from his hand, caught in my glass.

Empty in the Sleazy City

Where we go, the room tufted as alfafa
I am stuffed like an old mean parrot
in my wily corner, scarcely able to squawk.
And then I put on signs of my station
torn net, ripped stocking, a tinselled head
promising and full to overflowing; out bleeds
some small wound of straw, dry season.

And take to the streets full of wine's buzz
trying to grab the sky; but the words fall
unaccomplished and full though this is, my city
sifting its populations through the mind's shell,
yet there is no word, it sticks and roots
below the belt; my leg grumbles on its perch
my hand scratches at the pelt, its cushion.

I am well fed, the adverts tell me so.
The way my belly swells with its hoard,
the way I gobble up the colour and the seed.
Dance to the fullness of time say the people
(who are also tenanted and do not know
language of the night sky, stars' ignition).
The sleazy city presses oil and company upon me.

Where we go, ducking under the avalanche
of words, to where one single squawk or moan
rifles the city looking for twin; to where
the echo thrills behind the siren, satin
and broken shoe; the same cry spirals out
from empty women spread-eagled below bridges
and the man who says I also carry silence

like a gun to the same sky.

Reducing the Dose

Sometimes the air alone is enough to send
you flying, as though someone split the fruit
and spat you out, a gnarled old peachstone
rattling across salty seafront paving-stones;
no destination. The pier's an arm of oil and glitz
all its wares thrust and bursting out of booths,
kiss-me-quick, prize-every-time stall holders promising,
promising just like the barmaid in the Bath Arms
who's spilt her bosom into the counter's froth of beer
and dangles there, sending you silly with the memory
of home, more push-and-shove back there than all this
box of tricks, a seafront shattering its glassy hold.
And you've been wrapped for decades in soft flesh
staying tucked-up and dreaming in that cave, like Plato
witnessing the shadow-play of limbs juggling their
chances and mouths pronouncing futures you can't catch.

Last night I sliced a quarter of him off
working precisely with the kitchen knife,
knife-point chipping at this minute bomb of blue
as though I'm sorting through old clothes to see
what fits – discard the comforter, the fleecy bodice
and the belt; a pale-blue powder falls and dies there
in the saucer. My blade has taken him for less
and when we twist in love, a quarter-section of me
disconnects and rises from its cramp into fierce air
(the benediction) carrying me like a riddled stone
to the water's edge; a brain, a walnut newly-shelled,
its surface cavernous and lodging in the shingle
or any damned place where the world's blasphemy
erupts into your ear and strangers offer up their
                            gap-tooth smiles.

Farewell to Brighton

All that shingle ringing against its mate
and the sea overlapping into her thighs' fork.
She cases the pier, left behind when dawn creaks in
and celebration dries like an old prune
nobody's choice of breakfast.

And all the landladies close their doors
in a ricochet along the front
saying no, no, in a great chorus of squawks.
The parrots bite her fingers saying 'pretty'.

It is a long time, the pier was always thus
never without its damp undertow
a great fall-down from that bright stair
to paradise, a ruff of pink at the waist
a high white shoe; all tumbled, scuffed
and wanton in the bleary drift of moon
when dawn washes it, the sky scouring
her seafront sutra, her pink net petticoat
awash through all its wires; a long time.

All that shingle; still the stones mutter
against tides, against her heavy dream-swell.

Slowly they leave, the song's belovèd
the one who sang it out; going north or west
leaving the crazy pier, the change machine
the frantic rattle of a seaside town counting
                                        its cost.

VI: FEVERS

Un-Fairytale

After the wedding, frog leapt
   gladly back into his skin.
The mirror splintered when no face
   of hers shone there.
The lady of sighs let down her
   long gold hair
And waited, as the centuries
   crept past her window.
The princess and her prince slept
   unmolested by fruit.
Giant grins like an early
   species of baboon
Spitting his curses playfully
   from the clouds like pips.
A splinter in the bridegroom's
   heart was a mother's
Vengeance, and was not sent by
   the fleshless snow-queen
On her way north, that's a dead story.

They all rise up again
   miming and flickering
That dream army where the child
   once guessed the
Trick, that all was for sleep.
   And waking is like
A pond's split surface, like
   the skin her love
Creates for her now when he touches
   it, and she opens
And arranges herself, not at all
   tidily, into the story.

She Tries

She tries it many times
flaps at her wings and oils the carpet with sweat.
It pours rivers through the boards
and still she is floorbound.

She is a crow. A plain bird.
Ninety-nine blinks of a black wing
won't fly her. On the floor
are rusty chalkmarks; she needs
to get very close to read what
they say, they are so familiar.

They keep her caged upstairs;
the lining is torn on the living-room
curtains where she tried to get out.
She has raven's hair and they say
she's too old to wear it loose like that.

Sometimes a song will ooze through
the pores of the house and her
croak is of joy. Then she has
carved an arc to the ceiling, there
are a few feathers where the plaster cracks.

August Thief

She strips the house of its peeling paint and
it is white and boney like a man with no
fruits.
She strips the washing-line of shirts and
there are only phantoms chattering in the
wind.
Looking for cores, she peels apples until
they are bled.
Coloured confections fly from her cupboards
like wild confetti after the hunt.

She peers under the skin of a water-bubble
let loose from the mirror, looking for
captured storms.
She hunts another season's flower, folded
upon itself.
Until the house is twisted like a huge
spiral screw and the plants are etched into
graffiti on the stone wall, and the washing
is forged into metal arabesques and the
white lid of summer is closed shut over
her head.

Cut-Glass Punchbowl

Looking into water
she's watching goldfish speckle
the impatient core of afternoon.

Her face comes back
stripped of its oval, the chin
is jutting terraces of bone.

Her eyes multiply their flaws
sparking fish-shoals.

She's singular, one too few,
her two eyes hammer
at the thickening glass, cut
like a slithery waterfalling skirt
down to the square bald root
bearing all names of fish.

Too many, she's hooked them up
sounded them on her tongue
her heels on the wooden chair-rod
itching to fall.

*

Is it dog or human
howl tunnelling the street
flying us back
down our avenues
leaping back to the bone.

Like a great mouth
the cry swallows us back.

Her face is a patchwork
crimson flower, livid as glass.

The bowl fell about her ears
striking the ground like a bell.

Fish wriggled on the slabs
dying in shoals, slipping easy
through her cut-glass hands.

*

He broke the goldfish-bowl
over her head, calling her slut.

She wriggles the dying street
like a fish out of water.

The cut-glass fishbowl spends
its river, the creatures gape.

She takes her shards of crystal
to a neighbour's door.

In their gardens, people stir
and turn hot memories under sun

like plate-glass, dreaming of rivers
voice of another lazy fish

cracking their bowl, he broke
the goldfish over my head

she tells her neighbour
a slit in the cut-glass door.

Fevers

Cold Fever

You bring me ice, a winter fever
pressing tight across our pitted track

Even the name of you migrates north
like the crazy frost-bitten birds

In winter the telephone stretches
a thin arthritic needle into my ear

I hear flesh-whorls writing their
fevers in the lane's icy rut

Our skins mutter in their coats
You wait in a lace of ice

I'm leafing through hills, hunting
for voices in this cold pearl shell

Sounding the Fever

The trick is to know fever when
you smell it, see where it smoulders
in the pale shed-skin of ash

The trick is to know not where
we're going but the path's hinge

The hours scrape through; I rake dust
talking to you who called up tricks

you in the rain leaving home
(I don't say departed)

I'll send pockets of ash, urn-droppings
in an envelope, captured trash

The fever growls, cowers in a grate

Read it again, you've not understood
not lanced its heart, read it again

Writing the Fever

He throws his sex around then goes
to bed, she said adjusting a strap

You poets throwing it around
You asked for it, he said

After the Fever

Weaving us all piecemeal
through the hour called wolf

he hosts too many star-struck
stories in his stringy web

Voices leak through the
toss and pitch of eyes

and morning finds him fickle
still, and blind in the old chair

his faces gone, the pages
cling like petals to his knees

Zodiac

She is dying to lie down with the sun and the fish
except that Caroline insists on mimicking the flowers
cupping each camomile, excavating poppy
rescuing the heart of each burst marigold.

Three times they circumnavigate the garden
its pavings tip and crack letting earth through
until she's swimming with him in a bowl of light
turning the garden round and round in her crazy eye.

No fish, she's stuck back with the bull
hoofing it around the garden after Caroline
naming the signs, calling the lost flowers out
giddy with love, until her friend's tears fall

and stain the red silk blouse; and then
his name snaps and spills and out she swims
for Caroline, out of abundances of afternoon
into an ancient wicker chair creaking its bonds.

She's landed on a hot slab drinking tea
holding the sun down; it's Thursday afternoon
the book's unmade, the words are gritty;
too soon for bellowing of love

or slipping easy, easy under his scales.
The tears of Caroline fall through her own fierce
course; and lion matches sun, turns out of water.

Making a Season

I wasn't thinking of snow-hunger
more of a fragile flower-head nodding
stealthy out of its envelope.

My love's a book-length hawkish river
twisting its course. We read trees there
hear where the season drives the raven's croak.

Summer's easy; it's the stab of the north star
sharp as needles launching a constellation.

Keep your careful seeds, I'm sparse
as crab-apples in a lean month, holding
the source of rivers underground.

And going home I pluck the sweet
barbs out, skin catching its map.

Not snow-blind, mad on the rampant river
but hoarding where the land grunts
under keel and water, shoving roots on.

VII: CONCERNING THE ALLOTMENT

Concerning the Allotment

If I think of parsnips it is not to say
I am content with some ordinary vegetable
though the day
my neighbour left that bulbous root
propped against the step without a signature
I must confess the chain reaction
led to you.

I have been more in love with aubergine
a glossy flesh, an obscure bloom.
Eating that hybrid I've a whiff
of old Majorca way above the treeline
and castanets rattling against the ear
the rasp of more exotic fruit
in spite of you.

Going to pot you said, waving your pipe
sending smokerings into the vacant air
and whether vegetables or the nation or
the whole shoot, I can't tell; only cling
to all that architecture we never crafted.

And we never did reach the end of the
garden, the haven of your potting-shed
though travelling the wide lands through
rifling olive-groves and bald high places;
never did make it into husbandry
raking the earth over at the far end
to pull this tuber out.

This vegetable-patch is where
our hidden city crouches in
miniature under the fleshy leaves.

Fault

The fault lies not in me, mother
nor in the part of you I catch in
passing, between one breach and another.

Your words a carousel that captures
my head for its hub, and painted horses
whirl about my ears, trapping the wind.

Among these storms, this battered planet
pleads for mercy; you showed me much of
force-fields and their deaths. Under-stair

are many left-behinds, an orange dress
that failed the sun, a husband likewise,
and all that shudder of a mealtime

race to get it right – the place-mats,
names, the riddles undergone, your purposes
as monumental as this hurricane.

I'll risk sleeping here, roofwards, close
to the storm's height; today I sat hypnotised
by cracks in paving-stones, writing in bad weather.

Crossings

for Ernie

Today is silence, not of words' death
although so much is spoken, laboured out.
You lie and fight for each dear minute's
winnings, life's small permission.

You rogue, you've cheated me by going
off like that, out of our circle
taking your war-stories, your warm brown
eye, the sidelong poke at laughter.

My love in the wings waiting to fly.
You won't mind will you if I take off
while you're much more than earthbound
marrying with clay, testing sparse breath.

I'll sing you out dear friend, hold
your knotted hand; and make fire
strong and good. But oh you should have
waited, even now crack in my eager wing.

The Company She Keeps

for Elsie Lucas

Called up out of the anniversary
the slowly clenching fist your body makes
gracing the marble slab, my voice
carves out the freezing air grandmother
once light as eggshell in your downy bed
now locked and knotted at some final gate
where even I can't knock, can only crouch
afraid and headlong at your foot. I trace
my last lips' track across your forehead
where the road runs into silence; blind
and cold, your bluest eye clamped shut.

Since then I've made you bird again
only to end the flight. I'm dense as winter
in your passing; your voice undoes me when
the sheet falls and my skin's cold glare
tests out its night. I part the curtains
beam you out across the garden's moonstruck stare.
I'm wrapped in absence like the coat you made
me, tucking up the hem; too large, you said
as now this night's undressing, naked stars.

Grandmother light as bird, your threads
that once stitched up my life unravel me.
Bitter on the tongue this day's excess
breathing-in lilac from your apron's cave.

Breaking Waves

Laughter over the coast's thin corridor of turf
where my aunt cast her net; you couldn't fish
deep in these waters, the string not finely meshed.
Most of that marine-life ghosted swiftly through
and she caught unfamiliars, her white laced shoe
cutting its heroine deep on land; where the wave crests
and falls, there she giggles her revenge. I drown
you she rattles with the chattering stones; her voice
breaks with years of sliding labels on to pickle jars
and hearing soft love-fingers probing each other's
cleft. And always behind doors or in the cool
flecked cavity beyond a waterfall, unwanted islanding.

Out of the City

A long day's journey into light.
Leaves fidget, the aunts are causing trouble
again telling their beads, knitting it tight.

Rumour has it that there's no land
at the other end; they say make sure
you buy returns, be careful of quicksand.

Sailors' skins chipped with tattoos for luck
we're branded with our ocean history.
The bus drips stale fear and some of it stuck.

Aunt Gladys rides up front shrieking her
master-joke; the day she met her sailor
fire-cursed, the ship went up in smoke.

Aunt Doris knew the pattern off by heart.
The devil fell she says, opened this cloven dyke.
She knits him scarlet where her threads drift apart.

Rap on the eye's settlement, the pages shake.
Aunts trembling at this bee-swarm's sudden blast.
The journey gathers on our skin, stings it awake.

Simone Dances

A quick twitch of silver.
Stars tumble her calf's black stocking.
And he ancient as leather
arches his chest with its pantomime
intact, snaps his braces, launches
his forty years and more
into the lucky space she traces.

Simone dances, her skins
erupt into his ears; lined in black
she drifts a tattered scarf to
bless his scars; his shoulders
wriggle in their middle age.

He croons once more with feeling
an old nerve teasing in his ravished eye.

VIII: LETTERS WITHOUT PAPER

Letter from the Terrace

A leaf hangs precarious, torn by wind.
I couldn't close the door last night
foot jammed on the step, wood-knot.

Lost your last letter in a
downpour, uncertain what to write.
The leaf falls, veins itch,
messages are dense and need decoding.

What did the bishop say
between the cups, sweat running
down his crease? It's too hot
in the stadium, the gate's locked.

Can't make it to the bone, stench
of bad news clogging up the story.

Trying to keep within the page,
can't find your letter
uncertain what to write.
Reading the news, how next year's
fashion will be out of Africa
(as if the jungle isn't rampant
here, spreading its crop)

Have you bought shoes?
The market's gone upriver.

Write soon,
consider leaves; this one
cuts across the frame
interrupts the bulletin.

Do you remember fairytales
the tinder-box and granny-wolf
growling beneath her cap?

Write soon, the story dips
into its cousin underneath, who's
much more likely to take up the plot.

Vendetta

The night too large for their feverish
expedition, a lost land of France.
They spent a week itching for touch
while plundering each other through.

She rattled in his ears like coming rain
and so it did, fell like the gravel underfoot
rasped like a single jagged stone against
his spirit, until the heel bled.

Behind a screen his mutiny, the monsoon
told it, spilled grotesque snakes like
portents in the path, a dozen silver sheaths
to wrap up rage; he will not decorate

her arm with bracelets nor win her
heart with snake-rings to his own.
Only the rain and a reptilian life
oozing beneath the door under his crack.

And that night late the scorpion hung
like a crucifix above the bed and where
they mated; he took a sportsman's
weapon, hammered at claw and tail

with the club end of racquet and razed
the beast to earth; until its head pulped
into the wall's stone and plaster fell
in chips taking the sting, the flesh.

He told me this; I could not guess the
size of it, what vellum hung between night
and his word. A crushed insect gnawing
at my heart all night, him quiet beneath;

the story passed between us like a blade.

Music on Victoria Station

– 18th February 1991

On Victoria station, crossing safely at mid-day,
the crowds of travellers are thrusting harder than usual
against the air, (as though it were thicker
than water and cluttered with obstacles).
In front of me, two tiny busy wheels
support a cello, drawn like a human silhouette
across the pristine floor washed clean of blood.
Her lowered eyes sweep from side to side
like a broom swishing the floor ahead of her
and the cello glides like a privileged guest
across the station, special envoy wrapped in a case,
glides without interrogation through
the mid-day air that cracks like glass,
air that bears invisible splinters and hums
with fear – as though this man here, this one,
(carrying his newspaper like a baton),
or that one there, his eyes a shield,
(as though short-sight will cancel everything),
might be your dear protagonist at the last,
that last-ditch stand when light goes out for good
and no more cellos will bell and ache
for you, and no more bows will touch and tease out
sound that rings and worries at your heart.

I follow the woman with that precious hollow
sliding intimate behind, close on her heels,
wanting us both to make it to the overture
as though we have been granted a reprieve,
can start the movement over again, a gift
of one more cello crossing the crowded station.
I am imagining the lift and breach of knees
as she embraces her familiar, while I am
tracking my belovèd in the aftermath, draft
one more day's magnificat in my letter's music
out of the blast and rubble of the southern station.

Power Houses of Lumb Bank

First I staked the terrace
swam in my borrowed scales and
landed in the Himalayan Balsam.
Again insidious draughts that some
call scent, sicken and set to flight.
We could not walk, our boots crunched
in the empty opium-invaded air.
I go indoors driven by weed, his season.

And Mozart winged his power across
the slabs (my heart a polished stone)
and bit into the cracks. You cannot
keep it out this world's wish;
between my eyes a humming dynamo of loss
cleaves to the unforgiven; at the piano
she webs me, won't let go and pushes up
the Balsam, that rampant bitter stem.

I can make poems out of ash and stale
wine, the sear of anger on my flank.
We hum among the power houses
sharing our hoard; and in the huts
coloured like honeycomb, we're cased
to hunt that fluid oiling limb and eye
and flooding through the cells; as though
this precipice were fed by bees.

Ship out of Water

or *How the Tailor Cuts Our Cloth* for *Geriatric Critics*

There's time he said, for improvement
in middle-age she's only just begun
but if she tries she'll make it by the time she's
sixty, if she watches how the Martians get it done.

His day a needle's eye, through it a world gone
lean; skimpy you'd almost say, this cloth won't
meet across our flesh, the cut's too mean.

We're squeezed like hothouse lemons to oil
this tailor's meal, sharpen his fibrous tongue.
Our histories need stitches, so he thinks,
our songs the blasphemy of seams undone.

An early death confines him to his chair.
From there he ticks and tracks and marks
the errant march of hair and thread
across a page, under his itchy scissors-blade

while we dare new disguises, kiss of
a claw, lair of the uninvented shade.

The Fiction-Maker

At night her stories trace out autumn hollows.
Miss Havisham's unshed wish, equally over-ripe
glowers in her heart's pit; the hooks and buttons
of that gown's frozen fall tighten the dress
against all enterprise. I read her grieving
over lace, poised at the groaning summit of the weave.

Pages turn, flutter their tarnished blades.
In the next edition she adds a cuff
to virgin black, a single button-pearl lies
frost-bitten, impotent at the throat.
She gobbles lace; rusty as history's crank
her voices mouth misericords lining the walls
of fiction's Petra, a well-thumbed bridal-suite.

Lodged in the page she bolts her head
into the shredded cloth. Too late to break
her shrines and expectations, to work on the hoof
and all the nerves out-reached; too many books
since she dared copulate on pig-fat and the
                              Black Mountain.

Figure-Flasher, You Been Here Before

On this side of the fence
coil of convulvulus, arch-parasite
strapped to its mate.
And here a woman's legs clutch
at the curling fleur-de-lys
of her white garden chair.
She's riding iron girders in
her heart in place of him,
gaping with grief; her pert breasts
triumph in their nests; I watch.
She was my mother once.

Beyond green lattice I have
squared my patch and planted
peonies at the core; they're
regular and stand their ground.
I work with numbers on a grid
for this is my profession. I'd
snip her honeysuckle buds from
their soft trespass on my wall.
Paving the way for progress I've
mapped a rectangle of stone upon
her twisting ankle where it hooks.

And when she lays her green and cool
flecked body over grass without
deceit, I count my blessings and my
peonies, clamp my eye down below
the wall's rim and subversive crevices.
And I will not go back. I have arrived
now at the world of numbers, flash
my clean equations to the screen,
hold off the sun and pare off her flesh.

Such is my death, it flickers
endlessly among the stubborn leaves.

Letters without Paper

You see mother, there's more to it than that.
He sat in a corner most of the night,
looked out of eyes that wore their hoods heavy.
I know he left his lighter, black slab on cloth
and babbled most of it and didn't call the taxi
when he should, the room all scarleted with wine.
But I don't mind you see his fingertip
of pain, that lightning on my thigh, such
brief and shocking lifting of circumference.

And then an old man who can't make it
to the sea without a hood, dark glasses
and her eye's soft ground to walk on.
Are you looking, are you is what he says
pacing his cave, his voices aiming at the light
clinging like lichen to his throat's walls,
the tunnel tight. And then my daughter's song
that cradles him through Hove, the blind
seafront, the land's exhausted beachings.

Mother they're all shored up and left behind
and can't cry with you there demanding ice,
pineapples and pristine faces, photographic
evidence and the nervy kind of conversation.

Transmissions overload my morning air
so you see mother I take the cab to town
forget to telephone, contact my smart alec
in place of it; then stalk the crazy pier
where couples wait for sun in February
side by side, their faces hung like daisies
to the sky. And mother why, when all that
house fell down did you not laugh for joy
and take a single brick, memoriam.

It's damp today, I need a break
a fix. I'm in the same boat mother
as you and all the rest, staring at
the fag-end in the gutter, wishing
the street would open up with song
and the right music, tuned to my
ragged spirit's pitch, exactly.

IX: A PROUD SHORE FOR LEGENDS

A Proud Shore for Legends

Well here we are again jumping up and down
upon the shore, eyes all at sea, gobbling
the sand this time (forgetting Malvinas)
dreaming of desert rats, Arabian nights
and all that head-gear. What a year
it's been for camels swaying through our
narrowest needle's-eye. See how our fingers
poke into every pie (greedy before the storm)
into the crack and lull of a sheltering sky,
an inflammation of the digit and the tongue.
And see how the little bastard inside us all
waves his tomahawk, his tommy and his rattle
for our team didn't they, haven't they always won?

*

The boy with a mission polishes his gun
watching planes soar like silk-moths
into that deepening black of where he's
banished cat's-paw touch and raspberry-cane.
For he's American and they have smooth-talked
him and tidied up his plot to put him straight.
All he can do is wait on the shore of sand
securely tarnished. And in his right hand
(silky on the gun) a lifeline leaps and jerks
across the palm then stops before the cleft,
dirt-riddled gulf between his finger and his thumb.

*

They don't tell, don't let on. The screens
of Europe and the USA have made him legend.
At nineteen he's the son of light, a mine
of interference; fuzzy lines upon a grid.
And soon the great lid of the desert-eye will
blink just once and out damned spot he'll go

lancing the wound that never can be bled.
Just like Miss Havisham's wedding captured
in a cobweb before the consummation. No, boy
they'll never marry nor stamp each other out.
But you'll be gone before you know it, and so
the story won't be told you see, the legend.